LEVEL
1

KU-078-216

Whales

Jennifer Szymanski

**NATIONAL
GEOGRAPHIC**

Washington, D.C.

Bryde's whale

Whales live in the sea.

Some whales can swim in warm water.

Bryde's whale

bowhead whale

Other whales can swim
where it is cold.

When some whales dive, their flukes go up.

flukes

grey whales

Then the whale goes down!

A whale can swim deep in the water.

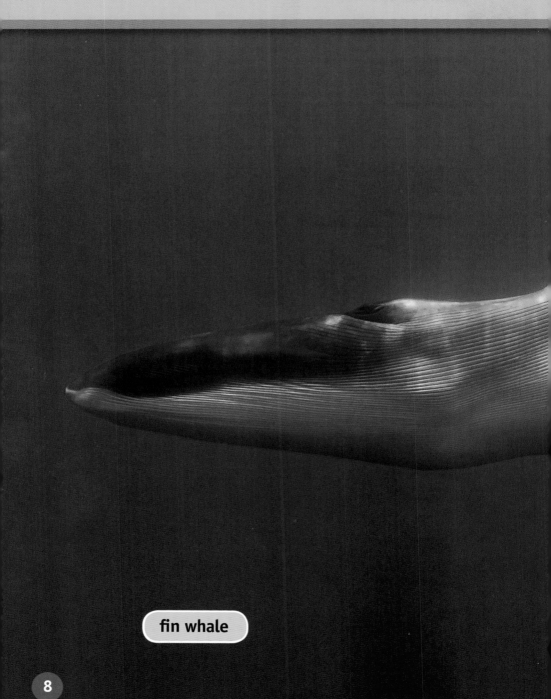

fin whale

Its flukes and flippers help it move.

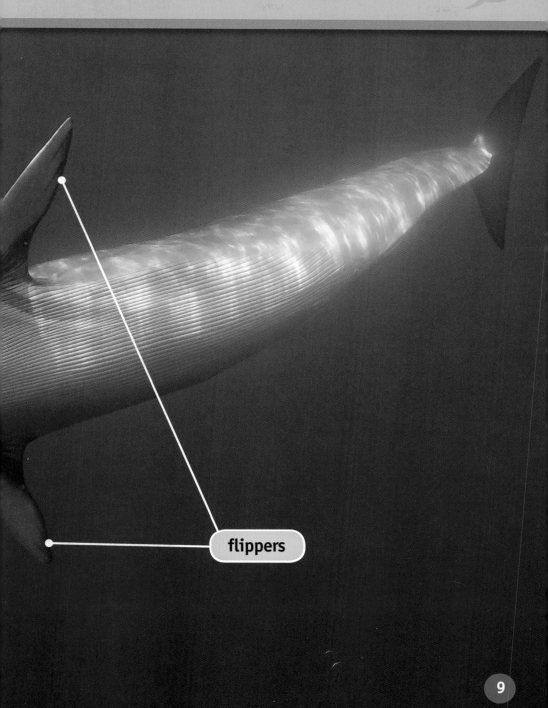

flippers

When the flukes go up and down, the whale moves forward.

humpback whales

Its two flippers help the whale turn as it looks for food.

These whales chase food deep in the sea.

sperm whales

They catch squid and fish with their teeth.

squid

Other whales don't have
teeth. They have baleen.

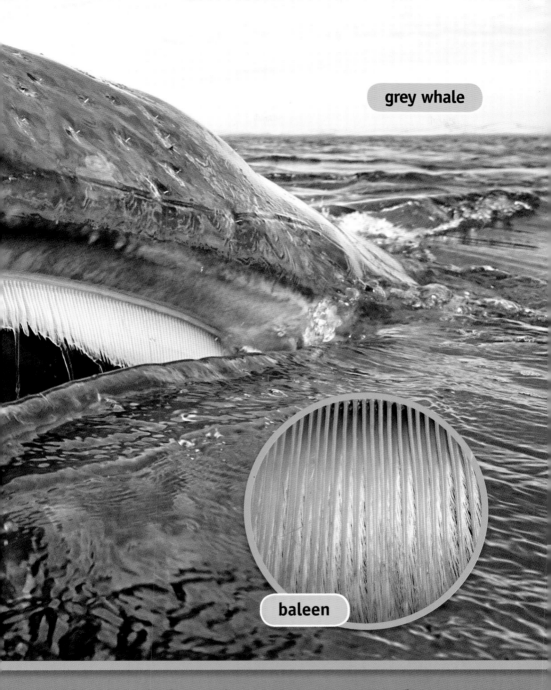

grey whale

baleen

Bits of food get trapped on the baleen. Then the whale eats the food.

15

Blue whales have baleen. They are the world's biggest animals.

lots of krill

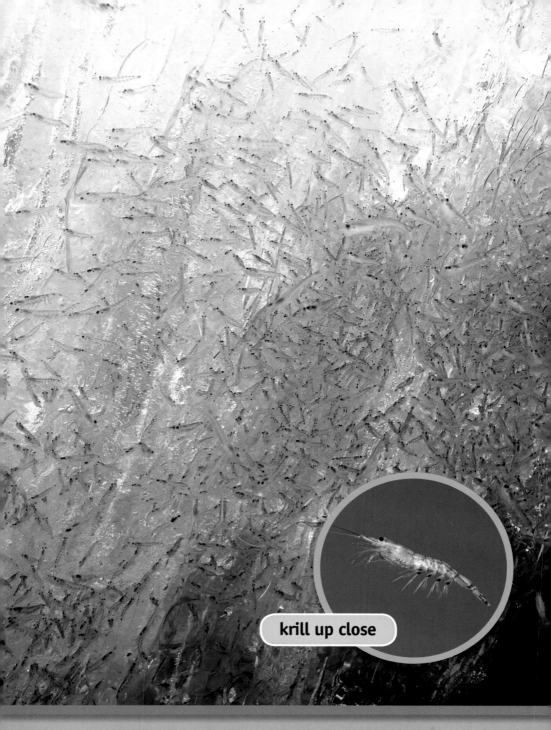

krill up close

But they eat krill, which is very small!

Time to swim up!
Whales need to breathe air.

humpback whales

Air goes out of a whale's blowhole. Then the whale can breathe in.

blowholes

humpback whales

It's time to play!

YOUR TURN!

How do baleen whales trap the food they eat? You can find out by doing this easy activity!

What you'll need:

small pieces of paper

a comb or brush

a bowl

water

What to do:

1. Fill the bowl about halfway with water.

2. Sprinkle the pieces of paper on top of the water.

3. Hold the comb or brush so that its teeth or bristles are pointing down.

4. Slowly move the comb or brush through the top of the water.

Did you catch any pieces of paper? Food sticks to a whale's baleen the way paper sticks to your comb or brush.

To Linda, who understands. —J.S.

southern right whales

The publisher gratefully acknowledges the expert content review of this book by Dr. Michael Moore, director, Woods Hole Oceanographic Institution Marine Mammal Center, and the expert literacy review of this book by Kimberly Gillow, principal, Chelsea School District, Michigan.

Copyright © 2020 National Geographic Partners, LLC

This British English edition published in 2020 by Collins, an imprint of HarperCollins*Publishers*
The News Building, 1 London Bridge Street, London. SE1 9GF.

Browse the complete Collins catalogue at
www.collins.co.uk

All rights reserved. No part of this publication may be reproduced, stored in a retrieval system, or transmitted, in any form or by any means, electronic, mechanical, photocopying, recording or otherwise without the prior written permission of the Publisher and copyright owners.

British Library Cataloguing-in-Publication Data
A catalogue record for this publication is available from the British Library.

NATIONAL GEOGRAPHIC and Yellow Border Design are trademarks of the National Geographic Society, used under license.

Designed by Gus Tello

ISBN: 978-0-00-842219-6
US edition ISBN: 978-1-4263-3713-0

Photo Credits
Cover, by wildestanimal/Getty Images; 1, James Michael Dorsey/Shutterstock; 2-3, Franco Banfi/Minden Pictures; 4, Doug Perrine/Getty Images; 5, Paul Nicklen/National Geographic Image Collection; 6, James Michael Dorsey/Shutterstock; 7, Michael Nolan/robertharding/Adobe Stock; 8-9, by wildestanimal/Getty Images; 10, WaterFrame/Alamy Stock Photo; 11, romain/Adobe Stock; 12-13, Tony Wu/Nature Picture Library; 13 (INSET), Franco Banfi/Nature Picture Library; 14-15, Christopher Swann/Alamy Stock Photo; 15 (INSET), Mark Carwardine/Getty Images; 16, Richard Herrmann/Minden Pictures; 17, Paul Nicklen/National Geographic Image Collection; 17 (INSET), Tony Wu/Minden Pictures; 18, Michael Nolan/robertharding/Adobe Stock; 20-21, Tony Wu/Nature Picture Library; 22 (UP LE, UP RT, LO LE), Hilary Andrews/NG Staff; 22 (LO RT), violetkaipa/Shutterstock; 23 (UP), Hilary Andrews/NG Staff; 23 (LO), Karen Debler/Alamy Stock Photo; 24, Peter/Adobe Stock

Library of Congress Cataloging-in-Publication Data
Names: Szymanski, Jennifer, author.
Title: Whales / by Jennifer Szymanski.
Description: Washington, DC : National Geographic Kids, [2020] | Series: National geographic readers | Audience: Ages 2-5 | Audience: Grades K-1 | Summary: "Information for children learning how to read about whales, with photographs"-- Provided by publisher.
Identifiers: LCCN 2019036141 (print) | LCCN 2019036142 (ebook) | ISBN 9781426337130 (paperback) | ISBN 9781426337147 (library binding) | ISBN 9781426337154 (ebook) | ISBN 9781426337161 (ebook)
Subjects: LCSH: Whales--Juvenile literature.
Classification: LCC QL737.C4 S99 2020 (print) | LCC QL737.C4 (ebook) | DDC 599.5--dc23
LC record available at https://lccn.loc.gov/2019036141
LC ebook record available at https://lccn.loc.gov/2019036142

Printed and bound in India by Replika Press Pvt. Ltd.

MIX
Paper from
responsible sources
FSC C007454

FSC
www.fsc.org

This book is produced from independently certified FSC™ paper to ensure responsible forest management.

For more information visit: **www.harpercollins.co.uk/green**